T0277593

AN ORDINARY LIFE

AN ORDINARY LIFE

poems

B. H. Fairchild

W. W. NORTON & COMPANY
Celebrating a Century of Independent Publishing

For information about special discounts for bulk purchases, please contact
W. W. Norton Special Sales at specialsales@wwnorton.com or 800-233-4830

Manufacturing by Versa Press
Production manager: Julia Druskin

ISBN 978-1-324-03685-2

W. W. Norton & Company, Inc., 500 Fifth Avenue, New York, N.Y. 10110
www.wwnorton.com

W. W. Norton & Company Ltd., 15 Carlisle Street, London W1D 3BS

1 2 3 4 5 6 7 8 9 0

I am proud to dedicate this book to the memory
of my brave, beloved son, Paul Fairchild (1970–2017),
lover and maker of comic books.

> *In brightest day, in blackest night,*
> *No evil shall escape my sight.*
> —The Green Lantern

Be kind to everyone you meet, for they are fighting a great battle.

—PHILO OF ALEXANDRIA

CONTENTS

AN ORDINARY LIFE

WELDER

My hood's lens darkens, a molten weld pool
boiling up in this portable green night
where I can feel, sometimes, beautifully alone.
The constant buzz and sputter of the arc
fills my head like a hard rain coming down,
and with the right stick and amperage,
a steady path of light begins to form.
Keep the arc gap tight, the angle steady,
and you're already headed home. No sweat.
My son, back from college, says welding
is alchemy (a new word for me), metal
grafted onto metal, *not* a living thing
but *like* a living thing, a new form given
to the world—not *your* world but the one
where I have a place, a craft, a trade, a self.
Handing me my hood as I leave for work,
he says, *You're medieval, a warrior, a knight
of the industrial order.* As a boy,
he would follow me on jobs, chipping slag,
the hard crust welding always leaves behind.
I work alone now. Work is who I am,
traveling day and night to oil rigs
and project sites in No Man's Land, sleeping
in my truck, rising to the task at hand.
Last night it rained, lulling me into a sort
of shallow sleep, odd bits of memory
and dream floating up: the radio's blue glow,
moon among the branches over Early Creek,
red streaks of tracer bullets on Saipan,

the jukebox of that honky-tonk in Meade
where my son recited from the last will
and testament of the poet named Villon,
and always, the rod's hypnotic whip and stitch
as I run an even bead with worn-out eyes.
It's not poetry. But it's what I do.
It's what I have to pass along in case
his poet's life proves not as lucrative
as he might like: my box of tools kept oiled
and free from rust, my steel-toed boots and fine
bronze cutting torch, a welding unit good
as new, and a pickup truck with a bed
where he can sleep, dream, ease the pains of work,
and rise again to make a life. *A life.*

ON THE SORROW GOD POURS INTO THE LITTLE BOAT OF LIFE

And God was there like an island I had not rowed to.

—ANNE SEXTON, *THE AWFUL ROWING TOWARD GOD*

I stand in the Punk Rock aisle of Rhino Records
mindlessly watching an old video of a Supremes
concert, trying not to think of anything, really,
giving myself to sounds from fifty years ago
that celebrate nothing now except my own youth,
my own Sixties when the world was ending
and beginning all over again, and it would be
all about love and the absence of war forever
once Nam was over, and the lies would stop,
and the boys would come back home, and Nixon
and McNamara and Westmoreland would pay
the price, and that's of course when it happens
and I can't stop it, *my son died last week,*
until the young woman standing next to me
bends down quickly, reaching to help pull me up,
and I try to make a joke of it, saying *Thank you.
You know, fifty years ago I would have asked you
to dance*, and she says, *Sir, I would be happy
to dance with you,* and so we do for a few seconds
there in the middle of the Punk Rock aisle, she is

so very sweet, *I am terribly sorry for your loss*,
and I thank her, and once again I know as if by
physical touch alone the innocence and kindness
of the hopeful before the world disappoints them
and it all seems like some awful rowing toward God
in a hard rain, one wave, one lie, after another, and
they are so tired, the oars so heavy, that they slowly
open their hands and pray and lean into the dark.

POEM BEGINNING WITH A REJECTED LINE BY W. H. AUDEN

We must love one another or die.
Or we can love and then die anyway,
the young soldier, laughing, liked to say.
In that small town, alliances with death
were everywhere: cattle standing in rank,
toxic feedlots; a well-tended graveyard
that expanded in proportion to demand;
the road from Epworth Hospital to the morgue
constantly in good repair, seldom blocked
against mortality or the ascensions
of the saintly dead—the ones who had not
fled the dust storms but stayed and somehow
held their farms against the darkening skies,
burnt-out crops, and topsoil blown for miles,
who placed wet cloths across their infants' cribs,
dug shallow graves, and spoke small, awkward prayers
for livestock that smothered in the heavy air.
And please remember Caroline Henderson,
who farmed wheat and taught Caesar's Latin
after evening chores, and German, to her only
child that she might one day study medicine,
who left the faith for lack of reason,
read Jefferson and Meridel Le Sueur,
and thought some saints, perhaps, were not yet dead.
She prayed in her angry, solitary way
against the dust and her daughter's coughing
through the night, yet somehow kept the farm

and loved the land in ways today we cannot
understand. And then died. From pure exhaustion
rather than pneumonia, her daughter,
Eleanor Henderson, MD, much later said.

MY MOTHER, ON HORSEBACK, IN A BLIZZARD

The black canvas cover claps and rattles
in the wind, her grip on the saddle horn
whitening her knuckles. She has lived
six years on planet Earth, and like other
children of the storm has been advised,
The horse will bring you home. Its name is Gray,
but for reasons known only to herself,
she, a country girl plain and simple, calls it
John the Baptist. *John the Baptist, take me home,*
she shouts into the wind. In the song of life
this will be her refrain in coming years.
The bruises from her first man, the savage
loneliness when dreams depart. The next,
the good one, gone for years in the Pacific—
one island, then another. The waiting,
flat and wide as oceans. The stories
that she tells her children late at night,
the lies she tells herself. The prayer, beginning
always, *John the Baptist, bring him home.*
And then, one fine day, the rumble, shriek,
and sigh of a returning train. The wives
in little bunches, their cries and chatter—
birds at sunrise, matins for the soul.
The fragrance of her blouse freshly starched
and ironed, the green one that he always loved.
The waiting. *John the Baptist, take us home.*

OFTEN THE DYING ASK FOR A MAP

So when Locie, embraced by the great softness
of bed #12, her late blizzard of silver hair
fanning out beneath head and shoulders, asked
for one in plaintive, almost desperate tones,
I went out to my car and brought back my old,
frayed roadmap of Kansas, and she followed
the unfolding as if it in itself were a miracle,
and then held it over her head, scanning
the red interstates and blue country roads
without apparent method or intent but
smiling her morphined grand smile of awe
and wonder within an air of childhood
surprise and overwhelming acceptance.
Because here it was—the way there, or here,
or out or over or in, and *here, sweetie,*
let me hold it for you, let me hold . . . and
her trembling index finger knows no certain
path but wanders through the Flint Hills toward
Cottonwood Falls, then darts up toward
Ossawatomie, and she can smell the new wheat,
its dark green deep as the jade of the necklace
her husband brought home from the war
in the Pacific. And now as she crosses
the Kaw River, she sees a young woman
standing beneath the moon in a wheatfield
in Kansas, and wondering, what will I be?
Who will I marry? Where will we live?
Will I have children? And if, at the end,
I am lost, how will I find my way home?

MILK AND COOKIES: THE COUNTY SEAT WARS

History is nothing but the activity of men in
pursuit of their ends.   —KARL MARX

His backyard was an undiscovered country,
an entire block of maple and oak in a town
without trees. Beside the winding driveway
lay a green pond stirred by Japanese goldfish
and a mermaid with naked breasts who spat
a perfect curve of water from her lips.
We stared at this awhile before we waded in.

He moved down on us the way a wounded sky
fell down on him in dustbowl days. We turned
and there he was: prehistoric, tall, white-bearded
as God's own self gazing down from eighty years
in No Man's Land: *Come in the house.* His wife held
cookies out, and milk, then pointed us below
where big-game trophies—great-antlered elk,
a bison's head, and rugs that grinned—were kept.

He told us stories: Beer City, thieves on the run
who hid out there, women who worked above
the Yellow Snake Saloon, then settled down
to raise *the bastards who built this town.*
He spat into a gold cup. A town without trees,
he said, and he brought the lumber in and

sold it and built *a goddamned goldfish pond*
and a mermaid rising naked from the sea.
Remember, boys, he said, *that history comes
down to this.* From a drawer lined with velvet
he took a Derringer and held it to my eyes,
then placed it in my palm: *I shot a man with this.*

ORNITHOLOGY

The young beg silently so as not
to attract predators to the nest . . .
this, passing before my drunken eyes
like the loose pages of memory, TV
staring through the darkened room,
shadows of Ukrainian bird life fluttering
against the wall of yellowed sheetrock
like Van Gogh's field of crows.
My uncle would have said, did in fact
say, *the paralyzed truth* for every lie
he ever told, truth in fact flying
out of the room like a thousand hawks.
We dream of flight, as he did,
but waking, blinded by the sun
smearing its fat lips on the one
unbroken window, find our feet
sunk in concrete, paralyzed, the truth
of our lives stuck like stones to the floor.
The young beg silently, their mouths
open always for the world's feast,
and then the song of the mother, sung
in terror and wisdom, and the paralyzed
hope of flight, the quick, awkward climb,
the fall, the wings loosening, giving,
the cat crouched low on the steady earth.

ALLEGORY

The price of life, my father said, *is $500*
in the state of Texas. If you want someone
killed there, and don't care too much about
the quality of the work, that's the price.
I was told this at the Petroleum Club
by someone who ought to know, and does,
and so there you are, college boy,
that is the world you are growing up in.
Don't ever say I didn't warn you. OK,
this is our old theme, isn't it? As in,
it's a dog-eat-dog world out there,
and I with my books and fine and noble
ideas, where certain lower things stand
for certain higher things, am simply not
prepared for it. Well, I do not eat dogs.
No, the dogs eat each other, but believe me,
one day you will order a filet mignon,
and they will serve you a dog. That's what
I'm talking about. Well, I won't eat it.
Yeah, you will. You'll have to, believe me.
And they will expect you to like it.

That morning, I recall, the rubber band
binding the newspaper had broken,
and its pages were scattered all over
the yard, blowing randomly here and there,
the news of the world wet with the dew
of a well-tended lawn in the corner of Kansas,
and I am thinking of the outstretched hand

of the assassin, and the softly spoken
but sincere *thank you*, as five new $100
bills, the ones with the beautiful blue stripe
down the middle, are laid there, the giving hand
careful not to touch the taking hand because,
well, you tell me. The wind never stops in Kansas,
always there, always pushing or pulling,
holding the front page of the *Southwest
Daily Times* flat against the screen door,
so I take it with me as I enter the house,
where my parents—good, kind, well-meaning
citizens—await the news of the world.

WHAT HE SAID, WHAT SHE SAID

When Candi Baumeister announced to us all
that J.D. was *in love* with Brigitte Bardot,
drawing those two syllables out like some kid
stretching pink strands of Dubble Bubble
from between his teeth, J.D. chose not
to duck his head in the unjust shame
of the truly innocent but rather lifted it
in the way of his father scanning the sky
in silent prayer for the grace of rain abundant
upon his doomed soybeans or St. Francis
blessing sparrows or the air itself, eyes radiant
with Truth and Jesus, and said, *Babydoll,*
I would walk on my tongue from here to Amarillo
just to wash her dishes.

                                There is a time
in the long affliction of our spoken lives when,
among all the verbal bungling, stupidity,
and general disorder that burden us
like the ragged garment of the flesh itself,
when, beneath the vast and articulate shadows
of the saints of language, the white dove of genius
with its quick, wild wings has entered our souls,
our immaculate ignorance, and we are,
at last, redeemed. And so is conceived and born
the thing said, finally, *well*—nay, *perfectly*—
or as it issued from the thickly lipsticked mouth
of Candi Baumeister, who said, *Well, babydoll,*
I've got a sink full of dishes. Why don't you wash,
and I'll dry, . . . and then we'll do it again.

BLACK FRIDAY

The handles of shopping carts are suddenly
slick with sweat, buyers' eyes bright with the fever
of purchase and possession—the sale on boat
batteries, for instance, whose contact points
promise both solitude and adventure,
the beginning of a new life. And the chrome
glamour of trailer hitches suggests, at last,
an end to loneliness. Driving home
at unlawful speeds, they will pass by
Meridel Le Sueur's PEOPLE'S COLLEGE
in Fort Scott, Kansas, where in 1934
the faculty called each other "Comrade"
and pledged allegiance to the lost harmonies
of the *Internationale*. Their children took jobs
in the Oklahoma oil fields, where roughnecks
were in demand and unions were extinct.
So here I am in the Wichita WALMART,
mourning broken farms, dying small towns,
the collapse of Jefferson's democracy,
the cheap, foreign, and properly shelved
goods of Black Friday, and reading
the tattered Oxford copy of Mandelstam
which, in the spirit of free enterprise,
I have stolen from the bargain bin.

THE WATER BALLET

From a balcony where Brahms spills from a speaker,
I watch the midday sun sprawl across this blue pool,
this chlorinated heaven whose clouds hang deep below
and darken near the end where the drain waits for winter.

Around the edge, legs dangling, our sons and daughters
murmur and fuss like new starlings fluttering among
spring trees. At some hidden signal, they stand, spread
their thin brown arms, touch hands, and fly into the sun.

AT A MEETING OF SCHOLARS I THINK OF AUNT BEA

Studies in attribution
wreathe the room
like fox heads around

my Aunt Bea's neck
in 1947.
Fox fur was big then.

So were Packards,
big bouncy boats
(ours was emerald green)

swaggering through Houston streets,
manned by fashionable dames
in fox-fur stoles.

And I sat swallowed
in the back seat, Packard
purring, fox heads flying.

She said, "Their eyes are fake!
They came from Marshall Fields,
half-price, in '38!"

I didn't care.
Deaf to dates and names,
oblivious to year and make,

I only thought of foxes
and how they lived
and what they ate.

MY ROOM NUMBER IS WRITTEN IN BRAILLE

below the useful Arabic
207 in black plastic.
Closing my eyes,

I brush two fingertips
against the raised dots,
and the door swings open

to the unseen and obvious:
folded towels, glasses sealed
in cellophane, a bed

wrapped tight as a gift
in brown or beige.
Eyes still shut, I resist

the immaculate embrace
of white tile, chrome,
and the TV's immense silence.

The ancient telephone, too,
and the directory fat
with the names of the world.

I sit still on the bed's edge,
feeling the air conditioner's
death-blast and the sun

slicing half-drawn drapes.

My hands slide across
the bedspread's patterned

rows and hollows, the far
country where my dreams
arrive, bright and visible

as candles held
in the hands of the blind.

KIMONOS

Late summer in that rented house,
dawn flung across the kitchen table
like scattered silks, morning's seamstress
obedient to the task of love, sometimes,
or other times desire, whatever fell upon us.

We wore kimonos, mine the one she made for me
only days before. Our hands would not lie still.
White tea, wind chimes, the cat's mew and cry
just beyond the open window, the way
she looked at me. What we felt, we could not tell.

The things they left behind: two blue T-shirts
with NAVY on the chest, *Vogue* magazine,
a torn paperback, Hersey's *Hiroshima*.
And then she asked about my father.
Yes, he came back. I began to brush her hair,

so black it made me think of starless nights
in L.A., the spray of city lights. *Yes,*
they called it LITTLE BOY. *So ironic, no?*
Wind moaned through palms. The rain
had stopped. I kissed her on her neck.

You were a little boy then. Suppose
they had attacked instead of dropping boys?
Branches raked the roof. *The first wave,*
well, he would have been among the dead.
The moon was down. We went outside.

How like dead people. To lie among the dead.
I've seen them. A street lamp flickered out.
I know. We said what we said, drank our tea
from ceramic cups, red with an undercoat
of gold, and my kimono, unraveling at the hem.

REVENGE

One day my father said, *Get in the goddamned car,*
and so I did, and he drove us about five miles
out of town, where he parked on an empty shoulder,
shut the Ford's engine off, and then turned to me
and said, *You have a weak personality.* I said,
What the hell does that mean? And he said, *You know,*
when you speak, the way you talk, laughing and using
all that fancy-assed, flowery language, you do not
impress other men, serious men, for whom life
is a serious business. I said, after a long silence,
weighing my fate for what I was about to say,
I don't give a flying fuck about impressing
other men. I can tell you, though, that I care
about impressing Patricia Lea Gillespie,
if that's the sort of thing you're worried about.
You read poetry, he said. *Yes, I do. I even*
memorize it. His eyes widened. *Why would you do*
a thing like that? So that I can recite it, I said.
Here's one that I recited to Patricia Lea
quite late just the other night. And so I began.
His car at that time was a two-tone rusted-out
Ford Falcon with a sluggish, nervous ignition, so
when he quickly reached for the key and turned it,
wrenched it furiously, swinging that small tragedy
of a car back onto Hiway 83, and headed for home,
I began, as I say, not just for the moment
but for all time and for all young men caught
in the rush of passion and sudden confusion
when the heart cannot speak but the man—oh yes,

the man—absolutely must, *she's so beautiful*,
the moon in platinum waves rippling down
her raven-black hair, and I rolled down my window
of that piece-of-shit car and I sang it out, far out
beyond the stalks of uncut wheat, beyond the corn
and soybeans, oh ever beyond the soybeans, and even
the beef cattle standing mute behind barbed wire
in a boredom so gigantic, so heavy it should
put God to shame, beyond Bryan's Corner where I once
saw Kerouac and Ginsberg and William Burroughs
stopping for a cheeseburger and fries on their way
to south Texas and future literary fame and
an almost endless supply of what native Texans
called Marihoona. My poem, I swore, spoken loudly
and very well as my father stomped the floorboard
with every burning word, would never end,
even after we hit the gravel in the driveway
at home and I finally leaped out and took a bow
for Dylan Thomas, and all of Kansas rose up
in the dry fields and applauded the art of poetry,
and Patricia Lea Gillespie later that night
gave herself to a boy who loved to read poetry,
a language so sweetly powerful and burdened
with the mysteries of the human heart that it became
my language:

In my craft or sullen art,
Exercised in the still night
When only the moon rages
And lovers lie abed
With all their griefs in their arms . . .

And I remember the grim, tight mask of his face
inflamed now by the porch light as he lurched
for the front door and I sang to Kansas poems
I so loved that they became a kind of revenge.

BENNY GOODMAN

> . . . *stories of a long-lost world when the city of*
> *New York was still filled with a river light, when*
> *you heard the Benny Goodman quartets from a*
> *radio in the corner stationery store, and when*
> *almost everybody wore a hat.*
>
> —"PREFACE," *THE STORIES OF JOHN*
> *CHEEVER*

My father was wearing a double-breasted suit
and green Homburg hat, and had just emerged
from the war in the Pacific, bearing in his arms
the chaos and nightmares of a thousand days
and evenings on Guam, Saipan, Tinian for deposit
in the First Methodist Church in Houston, Texas
where he would fall asleep in sermons preached
to aid his resurrection from a foxhole's grave.
But the stone would not budge, and he stood
with my mother for photos outside the church
and apologized for breaking up the Eucharist,
that Homburg resting in the sunlight like
a helmet or perhaps a halo starched and ironed
for Sunday service and lunch afterwards at
Gaidoux's. And, as I recall, one Ezra Brooks
or two or five too many. And my mother's pleas,
and then the sound of Benny Goodman's clarinet
all sweet and mellow rising from a nearby store

so that we all stopped on the sidewalk, tilting
our heads and just listening to Benny Goodman,
and then turning to begin the long walk home,
to begin forgetting, to begin, again, an ordinary life.

THE WATCHMAKER IN THE RUE DAUPHINE

after a photograph by Brassaï

Everything is so small. We can't even see
what he's holding or doing and so must take
the title at its word: he makes time.
And time—rows of gleaming pocket watches—
covers the wall behind the lamp where he works,
where the tiny watch parts and tools of his craft
are spread out before him. Night has fallen.
The Rue Dauphine and its shops are barely
visible through the window panes he will
raise his thickly bearded, wizened face to
now and then. The brightness of the lamp
shocks the darkness that surrounds him,
and when he glances up, he will see the boy,
face pressed against the glass between them.
The lamp is a sun. The boy is alone.
The Rue Dauphine is empty. A painting
looms above the watchmaker's shoulder.
His father? The man who deeded him the shop?
Who gave him a livelihood? Gave him a life?
Far beyond the watchmaker's shop, beyond
the boy and the ancient walls of Paris,
stretch the battlefields of Normandy,
the Atlantic ocean, the high plains
of America, and a machine shop
in a small town in Kansas, where a boy
studies under lamplight the bruised hands
of his father measuring out the last cut

of the lathe, the tools of his craft,
filing the burrs away while letting them
pop and hiss in the black water
and blue shavings of the gathering bin.
It is dark outside. The highway is empty.
And this is the world. All there is of it.

HOME

As always, it's the bottom of the ninth, bases loaded,
of course, and I, a weak hitter, reach far down
inside myself where Ruth, DiMaggio, and the great
though unsung Junior Gilliam live on, where
Bobby Thomson leaned into the one they still
talk about and all the saints chant in unison
their little prayers as I swing from the heels,
and BOOM! When I round second, the shortstop,
a true gentleman, reaches out to shake my hand
and offer the highest praise: *Nice hit, asshole.*
I lift my cap high above my head, and the crowd
shouts—no, *sings*—its hymn of praise from the top
of the Statue of Liberty: *Give me your tired,
your poor, your hitless.* I look into the stands,
and there is my mother hugging my sister,
who has somehow escaped the coma that was
her home for so many years, and my father holding
back the tears, and Aunt Vinna, home from the asylum
she never came home from, and even Uncle Bob
sober and sharp in a tailored suit and silk tie and
Florsheim shoes, flush with money and no longer
needing my father, and my cousin Tom Fairchild
back from the war in Korea where he left some
frozen fingers. Oh yes, they are all standing,
roaring me home, and as I cross the plate,
my wife, no longer arthritic, is two-stepping
with my daughter, who on the way to ballet lessons
would always sing, in her best country voice,

If you've got the money, honey, I've got the time.
And Jesus, there, look, stepping from the stands,
my brilliant, beautiful son, in his Green Lantern shirt,
so happy, and this time he will always be happy
for I am coming home and they all are running
toward me—my family, the fans, my teammates, too.
They are lifting me up, high up, toward heaven,
and so I wave my cap just as I did as a boy at my Lord
Jesus Christ and his mother Mary and all the angels
with their pathetic Budweiser beers and mustard-
leaking hotdogs sitting in the outer seats for we have won,
WE HAVE WON, and they all love me now, love me
for the fine and noble thing that I have done.

Well, the season of dreams is over. Boston finally won,
the Cubs three years ago, and my son's hatred of a world
where the only story is that somebody wins and
somebody loses has dimmed with the stadium lights.
I walk through crowded streets, listening to car horns
in the distance, a lone shout somewhere nearby,
the scuff and click of heels not far behind me,
people forever lost in the great puzzle of their lives,
going home, or wanting to go home, or perhaps walking
to the nearest bar, as I am, for it is for many a kind of home,
where the voice of Patsy Cline rises from the jukebox
and kind faces emerge slowly from the dark,
and I say, *hi mom, hello father, hello my excellent
sister, hello my doomed and incurably sad son.*

Seven Prose Poems from the
Journals of Roy Eldridge Garcia

THE HAT

At first I simply wanted something circular, appropriate to the region of thought, feeling, dreams, that life within life or the life that surrounds life, whichever, the problem is the same, escaping and returning to that which one can never leave, circling back to the origins that we felt were in the past but are in fact always revealing themselves in the future become present. So, a hat, a device of containment, a shield against most of what we can't see, a suitable housing for the movement of our lives, our heads bobbing up and down, going hither and thence in what we imagine not to be under our hats, namely the world. And each time we remove it, spinning, floating it through the air to take residence upon the sofa, or hanging it upon a rack, a hook, a doorknob, we marvel at its instantaneous reversion to thingness, a thing in the world far from our thoughts, our heads, perfectly and admirably useless. The purity of it: circularity without purpose. But then I discovered rain filling my hat recently lost and left on a park bench. As it lay there inverted and exposed, utterly reborn as a vessel gathering the most precious of elements, utilitarian and yet transcendent now in its human position, I rejoiced in such magic, such wondrous possibility, my hair soaked and my thoughts naked to the new life now thrust upon me.

He liked to hold them up to the full moon where they would fall and rise through silver ripples of light. Or, if held at a distance from the viewer, turn the night sky all liquid and glossy with stars. His mother had bought them years ago in the little gift shop of the Metropolitan Art Museum as a wedding gift for a friend but then had decided to keep them for herself. Usually they sat above the piano, but someone had apparently moved them, and their absence, however temporary, was causing him enormous anxiety. As a watcher of things, of mere objects, whether common or unusual, he prided himself on an innate ability to construct narratives about them. How they lived their lives in the glass world, the only world, after all, that they knew. Their glass parents and glass upbringing and beautifully transparent glass religion where nothing was hidden and everything could be held up to the stars. He would imagine whole novels where the glass children grew up and fell in love, and peering into their glass lovers, saw with marvelous clarity the infinite spaces and depths and distances within their little glass bodies and glass souls. This continued far into the night, and when his imagination began to fail, to tire and falter beneath the weight and mystery of this glass world, all he could do was put his hands on the piano keys and begin to play. And as he played— strange little broken melodies of his own invention, a little like Erik Satie, but awkwardly improvised—he looked up, and there they were, his glass children, returned to their places among family photographs and small ceramic vases and figurines, and of course he imagined them to be happy, filled with silver ripples of light as if they were falling and rising, as if they had discovered again their appropriate positions in the glass world and could never be, and here he paused, looking for a concluding tonic chord, broken.

PROPHECY

Jason was convinced that he could be a prophet if he just put his mind to it for he had always felt that he was living his life about five seconds ahead of everyone else. He began to think this way at Parris Island during a marching drill when his drill instructor informed him by shouting only two inches from his eardrum that he, the D.I., had obtained sexual congress with Jason's sister at her convent over two hundred times. At that moment Jason was watching two seagulls in the distance flying in intersecting paths as they ascended and then abruptly dove down, one going right, the other falling left. In the background was a row of palm trees forming a solid green wall behind the perfectly symmetrical flight of the seagulls. Somehow all of this, as precisely balanced as Bonnard's nuns kneeling in their white wimples on green lawns, reminded him of his friend, a field surgeon in Korea, who loved Bonnard and said one day that the strongest argument against the war was that terrible sound the zippers made when the body bags were secured. What did this have to do with foretelling the future, or with time in any form? It was this: he knew that tonight he would drop into his bunk exhausted, quietly and quickly say to himself the Jesus Prayer that he had learned from his sister, and then slide into dream-filled sleep where the seagulls would appear once more, one going right, the other falling left. And at some point he would hear the sound of zippers, thousands of them, until he awoke, shaking and mumbling uncontrollably, a few seconds before the rest of the platoon.

MARIO

Mario takes long walks at night, and when he sees a lighted window, he is compelled to imagine the scene within. On this night, he imagines a tiny, grotesque man with a large head resembling that of a rodent, who wears a yellow and lime-green plaid jacket and carries with him always two flying monkeys, one on each shoulder, named *vagina dentata* and the Penis of Rage. He has black fingernails so long that they curve inward and scrape the pavement when he walks the streets of his neighborhood, causing the residents to shudder and whisper curses. But when he passes a house with a lighted window, he, like Mario, pauses and imagines the scene inside: on this evening, an ordinary man and an ordinary woman who each night embrace, and the man says, *I will never leave you*, and the woman says, *you are my life*, and then, holding hands, they walk off to bed.

Each night as Anne drifted slowly into sleep, she permitted herself to see the GANO grain elevator as a magnificent cathedral rising above a tiny European village. She saw the asphalt main street under rain, the pink and blue reflection of the only neon sign in town, how the headlights of Leon Welch's Ford pickup became two luminous whales passing beneath the street's surface, the great inland sea of Kansas. At the west end of the street, Bud Neely's hardware store with its dream of No. 4 sandpaper and a bucket of semi-gloss. The Mobil station where elderly Mr. Andrews was robbed of thirty-seven dollars and closed the next day. Dwayne's Good Times Tavern, where no one had ever dared to, and never would, enter the men's restroom, where Mr. Andrews shot himself.

Her husband, Tom, lay in bed beside her, staring at the stars she had painted on the ceiling and listening to the litany of sighs from semis down-shifting along the highway. All those spaces between the stars. That was the romantic part. Those distant headlights, the stars themselves. That was just the sex part. When Tom reached over to hold her hand, she thought of him as a young man with his buddies working combine crews north as far as Canada, shirts off and deeply tanned in the photographs he sent home.

Last Sunday at All Souls over in Bethel, the priest's sermon caused her to think of the resurrection, the mystery of it, and her difficulty trying to imagine it. But she loved the simple phrase *Jesus rose* because it made her think of Jesus as a man, and that made her think of Tom in the photographs. Oh, to fall in love with a man named Jesus Rose. Mrs. Jesus Rose.

SPATULA

I had this friend who had a nervous tic I guess you would call it, whereby if he heard the word "spatula," he would turn and bite the person nearest him. I have no idea, that's just what he did. But the word "spatula" is pretty uncommon, so most of the time, no problem. But this one time we were sitting in a restaurant booth, and someone said, the way you will, being funny or smart-assed, "Oh, bite me," and my friend started crying, really wailing, gushing, it was horrible. Clearly, I thought, the antidote here would be to shout "spatula," but then you've got the biting thing and maybe an assault and battery charge, who knows. I thought about backing away and shouting it as I went out the door, but, well, cowardly to say the least. Kind of funny, though, a guy shouting "spatula" in a restaurant. But then how about "egg beater" or "blender." So many people in the world, that could very well be happening somewhere right now. At Kevin's Big Burger in Clyde, Missouri, "Egg beater!" and somebody's got a sore shoulder and that look of surprise on their face that really makes you want to laugh. But you don't. That would be impolite of course. But you want to. What kind of animals are we, laughing at other people's pain? What my pretentious English professor called "Freudenschaten," "Schadenfreude," who gives a damn, I certainly don't, I was just thinking about *my friend*. So, long story short, I said "spatula," and he stopped crying. But that's what friendship's really all about, isn't it? Your friend's crying, and you know what needs to be said, you know the word and he knows it, too, but doesn't want to hear it, but you say it anyway because you have to, somebody has to, somebody has to bear the pain, somebody, it's the only way, and there you are at the doctor's office, and he's saying, in a state of shock, "My God, man, those are *human* bite marks."

THE MEETING OF THE BOARD

Their arms lie along the table. The gold rings with their elegant settings shine like the eyes of infants. Or their own eyes when they sit zazen chanting the dulcet tones of *no tax on dividends*. The second hands of their watches plunge forward into the heart of the day, the mercilessly slow collapse into night, day, night, etc. Their fathers weigh heavily upon their backs, but the acquired grace of mercantile demeanor renders the daddies scarcely noticeable. One of them says, "My daddy is scarcely noticeable." Another opens his briefcase. "Mine neither. It's been a good year." With the mention of the word "year," their eyes pivot noiselessly toward the wall calendar where a young woman in diaphanous clothing kneels within the oval of a tractor tire. "Some sweet melons there," says one of the board members. "Yes, those are finely sculpted features, accomplishments we can all be proud of," says the one with the briefcase whose golden latches catch the bright ornaments of the sun. The meeting proceeds, and soon a lavender hush descends upon the room. All that can be heard are the whirring of second hands and the low rumbling of the voices of commerce: the give and take, the gentle reply, the fond, delicately couched interrogation.

INWARD

There is another world, and it is inside this one.

—PAUL ÉLUARD

The scrub oaks beyond my window
slipped, tree by tree, into fog,
ice lacquering the black branches
that dipped and clattered in the wind
making random flashes—the flicker
of street lamps in Paris, perhaps,
or the Gauloises of crowds at the Dome
with their red wine and blue copies
of *Ulysses*, like fires along the Seine.

The fog lay on the plowed ground
of my grandfather's farm that rolled
and blundered through low-lying hills
and gullies to a dusty creek, damp
only when winter wheat was bogged
in snow. From my bed, moored among
bubbling vials of medicinal ethers,
I would wander that creek, winding
among bunchgrass and ragged mesquite,

wander its length, inward, standing
at last high above the great cities
of Europe and their thousand lights
rising through the layers, secret

and deep, of dusk in winter. Now
was the leaving, the motion inward,
my task, my hunger, to wake from
the thickening air of sickness, to walk
into fog and the world inside the fog.

GROCERIES

If you stopped moving, you froze.

—NED FORNEY, "THE BATTLE OF THE
CHOSIN RESERVOIR"

for my cousin Tom Fairchild, USMC, 1951

The dropped can of mushroom soup thudded dull
and flat, the way grenades did hitting frozen earth,
Tom said. The old man was ancient, maybe timeless,
hands mere clubs of flesh, no thumbs or fingers,
as he reached for it, so I held it out, waited, then
placed it gently in his cart. He just nodded, turned,
and quickly moved toward the dog food, chips,
and TV dinners. He still wore the old field jacket,
semper fi, buddy, my God, from sixty years ago,
patches everywhere, thread-bare, faded and darkly
stained *from what,* I wondered, and standard issue
boots resoled twenty times or more, I'd guess. The way
he tried to hold the cans would break your heart,
childlike, really, one stub on top, then on the bottom,
sliding it quite cautiously, as if it might explode,
then placing it between the others in the cart,
neatly, in a kind of military order, rows and ranks.
He was slow, scanning section names overhead
the way perhaps he once would search the clouds
for MiG-15s, squinting, waiting for the sky to clear.
Pausing to admire the rib-eye and sirloin steaks,

he pushed right on to the day-old bread and bargain
beer, *Old Milwaukee, Bud,* and the bourbon stacked
along the bottom shelf. And when at last I reached
to help unpack his cart, he pushed my hand away
and stared hard into my eyes. Hard. *Get the fuck
away.* I had heard Tom tell my father, *grown men
calling for their mothers.* Outside, rain pummeled
the asphalt, a cold wind pushing from the north,
the old man turning when I spoke, *You were there,
weren't you?* I raised my hands, fingers spread.
Chosin. He smiled and looked away as I held the door.

THE FIRST WORD

Drifting through the salt air, it begins as a toneless
rush of pure breath, rather like a long sigh or gasp,
a surprise to speaker and listener alike,
the parted lips, slight tremor as it's repeated,
hand raised in a hollow gesture now that sound
suffices, the rounded, childlike eyes, and at first
an "oh" or "ah," not a word but just one more
dumb, inarticulate defense against the future,
the vast, dark unknowable, until the arrival,
heaved and halting, of what was later
called the *whisper*, a word that sounded like it meant,
actually performed itself in being said at all, *whisper*,
and so was considered magical and somehow
the reason for all the words that would follow
in such profusion, a river of words flowing
from that first whispered word, *help*, and again, *help*,
and then, *help me God, help me please*, and *baby,
you've got to help me*, and then, swelling to a flood,
*they want the money and they want it now,
help me for God's sake*, and *I'm so sorry, sweetheart,
I need help, I know that*, and later he's on his knees
at six in the morning and whispering a whole
thesaurus of words into the hard, brittle
morning light. *Help. Oh sweet Jesus she's
gonna leave me. Help, help me, I need some help.*

FOR JUNIOR GILLIAM (1928–1978)

In the bleak, bleacherless corner
of my right-field American youth,
I killed time with bubblegum
and baseball cards and read the stats
and saw a sign: your birthday was mine.

And so I dreamed: to rise far
from Kansas skies and fenceless outfields
where flies vanished in the summer sun.
To wake up black in Brooklyn,
to be a bum and have folks call me Junior
and almost errorless hit .280 every year,
and on the field, like you, dance double plays,
make flawless moves, amaze the baseball masses.

You would turn, take the toss from Reese,
lean back and, leaping past the runner's cleats,
wing the ball along a line reeled out
from home and suddenly drawn taut
with a soft pop in Hodges' crablike glove.
And we went wild in Kansas living rooms.

The inning's over. You're in the shadows now.
But summers past you taught us how to play
the pivot (or how to dream of it).
And when one day they put me in at second,
I dropped three easy ones behind your ghost,
who plays a perfect game.

MY FATHER, FIGHTING THE FASCISTS IN WWII

The words of the prophets are written on the
subway walls.   —PAUL SIMON

The old guy on the A-train uptown said,
Read some European history, college boy.
Believe me, they'll be back. Voices from
the earth. As always, wisdom from below.
My father, high school dropout, in a flooded
foxhole bailing water with his helmet
while his buddy out of CCNY explains:
History repeats. Believe me, my friend,
up to your ass in the mud of war, the foes of
democracy always return. Always. The modus
operandi will be power for the sake of power,
suppress the vote, attack the free press, ban
books, always lie, and something I will call
epistemological terrorism. Tell your son,
for it could happen in his time. My father
hands him his copy of *Dubliners*, now ruined
by rain and cowshit covering the pasture
they had just taken. *Ah, poor Joyce. Poor*
Truth. The Death of the Word when Truth
is the very mud we bail from our grave.
The rattle of machine-gun fire in the distance.
Flares that remind him of the fourth of July.
That madman, that German sociopath

who caused all of this. A cult of personality,
a kind of collective psychosis. Sunrise soon,
my friend. Koheleth saith so, and there is
nothing new beneath it. TELL YOUR SON.

TWO SONNETS

It was the only world he knew back then:
brown fields, oil pumps like great birds that rose
and fell, big-haired women, roughneck crews.
The rig lot sunk in mud when storms blew in,
and country songs that told of love and sin.
At night he stood alone on deck, the dark ooze
bubbling up, drill pipe grinding, a moon in trees
that shrouded it. Dirt, grease, the cold night wind.
The bunkhouse calendar displayed a girl, nude
and smiling, dark hair spilling down her back.
He had never known a woman, and never would,
he thought. *But now, ten years later, his bed*
grows warm, she snuggles close, and her hair, black
as oil, comes down the way he dreamed it should.

The sudden kiss, some awkwardness, the bar
of soap she drops onto the bathroom floor.
Would you, please? she asks, and hands me more
of something said to fill her hair with stars.
I love to feel your hands, your fingers, there.
As she looks up, the shower's heavy downpour
casts her as weather's orphan: the plumbing's roar
and thunder, clouds of soap-streaks in her hair,
her eyes, the look of children in a storm,
the ones too brave to run back home in time.
But soon the drops that diamonded her face
seem more like tears, and grief begins to form.
For that was long ago, and now I dream
of hair in rain. A girl I loved. A time. A place.

AN ORDINARY LIFE

an ordinary life with its taste of water

—ADAM ZAGAJEWSKI

I. The Son, Waking Early, Receives the Dawn

The sheet-metal sky of Kansas slides into morning
like the huge shop door hurling back a storm of light
that bludgeons the sleeping son, his stunned eyes.

Above his bed *DownBeat* photos of Thelonious Monk
and Charlie Parker explode into the blaze of dawn.
He slumps snail-like on the bed, asthmatic, tears

smearing his sight. Groaning awake, he scours
his eyes with rough, bruised fists and gulps
the dust-bowl air of drought and bone-dry creeks.

Yesterday childhood's truckload of Milk of Magnesia
was honking at his back, tires squealing, but now
he whistles "Stardust" to the mirror as he shaves.

At breakfast his parents dissolve into white cups
of coffee, bacon, pancakes. Later in the winch truck
he will recall a dream of home runs and double plays.

II. The Son at Work

In the shop, the lathes raise their dark hymns
while spirals of blue shavings settle into pools of oil
and water that bubble up thick vowels of steam.

Sleep lifts slowly from the khaki shirts of welders
and machinists as they hold their tin coffee cups
to their chests like little offerings, bright coins

bearing sunlight. Barn swallows bicker under
the tin roof when somebody's bit digs in, pulling
shrieks from threaded drill pipe. Welders in black

masks cut huge sheets of iron so loud the shop dog
begins to howl. Their bronze torches gleam like
knives, like swords, the son thinks, while he joins

two iron strips and chips slag from the new seam.
His radio announces New Orleans under hurricane,
and he hears whorehouse jazz flooding the streets.

III. The Son Meditates in the Privacy of his Chevrolet
Automobile

He drives a blue, raked Chevy into an absence
of trees, horizon pulling the sky tight, then torn
by a sudden cry of grackles. The highway is

a long prayer, and the car is a world, a life beyond
the endless fields of wheat and maize, *the known*,
crucifix and dice dangling from the rearview mirror,

droves of beer cans tumbling over the floorboard.
Everywhere the strange grief of telephone wires, radio
scattering metaphors for broken hearts from Del Rio

to Dallas. Everyone is dying for love: the son,
the women he dreams of, and Virgil, the welder,
who sculpts iron nudes behind the shop and offers

the son ancient wisdom in koans vague as dust clouds
blowing in: *a wise man knows, just by looking, whether
an animal is walking toward or away from water.*

IV. The Son Departs

He reads the brutal sun of high noon as judgment,
a refusal to forgive, and the pastures flowing past,
the cattle's stare, tumbleweeds caught beneath

the rear axle, fill him with guilt, so he throttles
the Chevy toward Kansas City, vowing to stand on
the corner of Twelfth and Vine before midnight.

The perfectly square, brown lawns of Wichita remind
him of home, the orange lawn chairs, black snakes
of garden hoses, and inside, the light and shadow

of TV in living rooms. The neon signs of motels
and burger joints brighten in the sudden rain, and
back at the shop, lathes wind down in great sighs.

The house he was raised in sinks slowly into dusk.
His parents chat in the orange chairs. The dust bowl of
Kansas darkens. Somewhere, oceans spill onto beaches.

ACKNOWLEDGMENTS

I wish to gratefully acknowledge the following publications for poems that originally appeared in them (although, in some cases, in very different form):

Beloit Poetry Journal: "A Small Town in Kansas," "The Glass Children"

Flight (The Devil's Millhopper Press): "Ornithology"

Hudson Review: "Poem Beginning with a Rejected Line by W. H. Auden"

Image: "My Mother, on Horseback, in a Blizzard," "Often the Dying Ask for a Map"

The Little Magazine: "For Junior Gilliam, 1928–1978"

Luvina (Mexico): "The Hat"

New Letters: "Allegory," "Black Friday," "Milk and Cookies: The County Seat Wars," "Kimonos"

RE:AL: "My Room Number Is Written in Braille"

River Styx: "Spatula"

Sewanee Review: "On the Sorrow God Pours into the Little Boat of Life"

Smartish Pace: "Home," "Revenge"

The System of Which the Body Is One Part (State Street Chapbooks): "An Ordinary Life"

Texas Review: "At a Meeting of Scholars I Think of Aunt Bea"

"Revenge" also appeared in *Pushcart Prize XLVI: Best of the Small Presses.*

I would also like to thank my editor, Jill Bialosky, for her guidance and for her patience during a difficult time of my life. My continuing gratitude goes also to these friends and comrades for all sorts of kindnesses and shoulders to lean on over the past few years: Bruce Bond, Patricia Fairchild, Sarah Fairchild, Jeanne Gillingswator, Chic and Paula Goldsmid, Frances McConnell, H. C. Palmer, John Peavoy, Wyatt Prunty, Dianne Schleiss, Maurya Simon, Nicole Smith, Richard Taylor, and Dan Ward.